INTRODUCTION SCIENTISTS MORALTY

JOHN LOK

ISBN 979-888569184-0

Contents

Preface

I write this book concerns to explain whether what are the moral differences between scientists and businessmen and medical doctors. I give ideas to let scientists to know why who need to concern moral and ethic when they are carrying on their science research. I shall suppose different situations to let these scientists, such as physical, earth, plant, medicine, computer etc. My aim is to raise their judicious ability to judge whether who ought or ought not follow morality to do their scientific research in any situations as well as whether who will encounter what of challenges if who don't follow the morality to do their research in the situation . I hope any scientists can learn how to deal their moral behavior to do correct scientific decision.

Prologue

Table Of Content

CHAPTER ONE

What is scientific morality

Morality (from Latin: moralitas, lit. 'manner, character, proper behavior') is the differentiation of intentions, decisions and actions between those that are distinguished as proper and those that are improper. Morality can be a body of standards or principles derived from a code of conduct from a particular philosophy, religion or culture, or it can derive from a standard that a person believes should be universal. Morality may also be specifically synonymous with "goodness" or "rightness".

Ethics (also known as moral philosophy) is the branch of philosophy which addresses questions of morality. The word "ethics" is "commonly used interchangeably with 'morality', and sometimes it is used more narrowly to mean the moral principles of a particular tradition, group, or individual." Likewise, certain types of ethical theories, especially deontological ethics, sometimes distinguish between ethics and morals: "Although the morality of people and their ethics amounts to the same thing, there is a usage that restricts morality to systems such as that of Immanuel Kant, based on notions such as duty, obligation, and principles of conduct, reserving ethics for the more Aristotelian approach to practical reasoning, based on the notion of a virtue, and generally avoiding the separation of 'moral' considerations from other practical considerations."

What is scientific research meaning?

Scientific research is a systematic investigation to establish facts. An attempt to find out something in a systematic and scientific manner. A systematic investigation designed to develop knowledge and a focused systematic study undertaken to increase new knowledge or understanding. It is the collection of information about a particular subject.

Why scientists need to concern morality ?

An enquiry that involves seeking evidence to increase knowledge. For a biomedical scientist example, who needs to share between different research disciplines, such as the need for some methodology, will be interpreted in significantly different ways. His research aimed to demonstrate the phenomenon of human conditioning by conditioning an 11 months old infant to fear rats by associating, then with fear inducing circumstances, such as a loud noise; biomedical experiments include freezing to induce hypothermia, infection of research subjects with malaria and tuberculosis (TB) and many consent of the research subjects and often leading predictably or extreme gain, mutilation and death. This issues are unmoral bad result. Hence, biomedical scientists need to concern whether whose scientific research is moral to society.

How to teach scientific morality to students?

For another example, biological scientific research, a mixed method design was to address the issue of effectiveness of ethical frameworks in enabling students to develop ethical reasoning skills in year 10 biotechnology program. This ten weeks program, focused a gene technology, genetically modified foods, genetic engineering and reproductive technologies. Each student attended to do experimental design quantitative data from the pre and post program questionnaires were used to determine the effectiveness in the use of the ethical frameworks. The questionnaires assessed the student's understanding and ethical thinking, attitude and opinions of biology scientific knowledge and ended with a section on the student's religious faith.

What is morality meaning?

Morality means manner, character, proper behavior" to be judged whether the scientist's behavior is the differentiation of intentions, decisions, and actions between those that are distinguished as proper and those that are improper by the acceptable standard of the society. Morality can be a body of standards or principles derived from a code of conduct from a particular philosophy, religion, or culture, or it can derive from a standard that a person believes should be universal. Morality may also be specifically synonymous with "goodness" or "rightness." Moral philosophy includes moral ontology, or the origin of morals, as well as moral epistemology, or knowledge about morals. Different systems of expressing morality have been proposed, including deontological ethical systems which adhere to a set of established rules, and normative ethical systems which consider the merits of actions themselves. However, immorality is the active opposition to morality (i.e. opposition to that which is good or right), while amorality is variously defined as an unawareness of, indifference toward, or disbelief in any set of moral standards or principles.

What is medical moralty ?

Beauchamp T. L., & Childress J.F. (2001) defined that "ethic is the moral reasoning of actions. For example , Why medical ethics is important? Medical professionals increasingly find themselves confronted with moral questions, e.g. ethic guideline address special medical services , such as blood transfusions and health services and health care for patients living with HIV/AIDS ethical issues that arise a clinical medicine. It addresses justice, equity and access to medical care. It also focuses on general duties of doctors, dentists and pharmacists."

For medical scientific research and ethic relationship, the global medical profession has maintained simple ethical standard for more than 4,000 years. the majority patients, physicians and other medical and health care providers often face ethical challenges, many of them consider ethics to be a concept pertaining to the avoidance and biology is referred to as bio ethics or biomedical ethics. Ethics is an intrinsic part of medical practice and shapes the medical profession and it must be implemented and individual behaviour of approaches that are based on someone's beliefs. Medical ethics isn't about avoiding harm, rather it is a set of norms, values and principles. These norms, values and principles are intended to govern medical ethic conduct.

Why scientists need to know ethics.

To answer this question, you need to attempt to answer these questions before you find the reason to answer this main question, such as below:

What is it to live a morally scientific research life?

Why is scientific morality important to carrying on researching?

Are moral principles valid only as scientists depend on their countries' cultural approval or are there universal moral truths?

How should scientists live in moral life?

Are there intrinsic values?

Which is the best moral scientific theory when who are carrying on researching?

Can scientists derive moral values from facts?

Is there a right answer to every scientific problem in life?

Which is the relationship of religion to morality?

Thus, I believe ethics in science is basic principles. In fact, science has a special role with respect to ethic, society demands high standards of scientists, it isn't always easy to determine the right thing to do, breaches of scientific ethics make headlines and ruin careers. Ethics have different categories. They include as below:

● Personal ethics: Morality .

Professional ethics: Standards & expectation.

Societal ethics: law.

● What is ethical standards? Should do the right thing? Should I do the right thing? What is the right framework for making ethical decisions?

As Gert., (1988) explained " ethic is a system of public, general rules for guiding human conduct. Ethics (also known as moral philosophy) is the branch of philosophy which addresses questions of morality. The word "ethics" is commonly used interchangeably with morality, and sometimes it is used more narrowly to mean the moral principles of a particular tradition, group, or individual. Likewise,certain types of ethical theories, especially deontological ethics, sometimes distinguish between ethics and morals."

Why do scientists need to know whether their behaviour are be acceptable to morality ?

I believe that science means the research is for truth, such as a quest for objective knowledge about nature; it is social institution means serving society's needs and improving people's lives as well as it made up of people with human needs and desire; and it is a profession, involving training, standards , a career, respect and privilege. Whether where is science done? Science is done at universities, in government, laboratories or government funding, in military laboratories or with military funding, industry laboratories or with industry funding. Scientists need to know different standards and goals apply to organizations under different circumstances. University goal is to advance knowledge to educate students to serve the public, government goal is to protect the nation's people and property to compete and cooperate with other nations to keep global security and to serve the companies or general industry, and increase opportunities in the global market. Hence, when any scientist works in different organization, then the organization will has different goal and the scientist will have the different goal and different scientific morality or ethic in different situation. Science include Astronomy, Biology, Botany, Computer science, Chemistry, Cosmology, Geography, Geology, Jurisprudence, Mathematics, Paleontology, Physics, Economics and others etc. different scientific researches. A scientist is a person engaging in a systematic activity to acquire knowledge that describes and predicts the natural world. In a more restricted sense, a scientist may refer to an individual who uses the scientific method. The person may be an expert in one or more areas of science. Also scientists perform research toward a more comprehensive understanding of nature, including physical, mathematical and social realms. Hence, Scientists are also distinct from engineers, those who design, build, and maintain devices for particular situations; however, no engineer attains that title without significant study of science and the scientific method. When science is done with a goal toward practical utility, it is called applied science. An applied scientist may not be designing something in particular, but rather is conducting research with the aim of developing new technologies and practical methods. When science is done with an inclusion of intangible aspects of reality it is called natural philosophy. Scientists are also distinct from engineers, those who design, build, and maintain devices for particular situations; however, no engineer attains that title without significant study of science and the scientific method. When science is done with a goal toward practical utility, it is called applied science. An applied scientist may not be designing something in particular, but rather is conducting research with the aim of developing new technologies and practical methods. When science is done with an inclusion of intangible aspects of reality it is called natural philosophy. Besides, Science and technology have continually modified human existence through the engineering process. As a profession the scientist of today is widely recognized. Scientists include theoreticians who mainly develop new models to explain existing data and predict new results, and experimentalists who mainly test models by making measurements — though in practice the division between these activities is not clear-cut, and many scientists perform both tasks. However, scientists can be motivated in several ways. Many have a desire to understand why the world is as we see it and how it came to be. They exhibit a strong curiosity about reality. Other motivations are recognition by their peers and prestige, or the desire to apply scientific knowledge for the benefit of people's health, the nations, the world, nature or industries (academic scientist and industrial scientist). Scientists also tend to be less motivated by direct financial reward for their work than other careers. As a result, scientific researchers often accept lower average salaries when compared with many other professions which require a similar amount of training and qualification. Hence, scientists are professionals, whose mission need to invent any new methods to solve any challenge, as human are encountering. It implies that who must need morality to do their scientific research to achieve benefits to human, but who can't earn extra awards unfairly from social assistance. Hence, scientists must need to know whether their behaviour are be acceptable to morality before or during they decide to do any scientific research.

I believe that different kinds of scientists need to follow their professional scientific moral standard to decide how to do whose scientific research. Because different situations will cause who have different moral view to do the correct moral behaviours, moral standard is no any correct guideline to conclude whether the scientist's moral behaviour is be accepted or not to do whose scientific research. Hence, any scientists need follow their professional scientific responsibility to prepare how to do correct moral behaviour before who decided to do any scientific research.

Finally, I shall indicate that why scientists needs to concern human genetic engineering science ethical and moral issue, it may seem of sience fiction, but genetic engineering has now entered the actual of human possibility. so, it is influenced to any patient's life risk. What does our science actually allow scientists to do today and what could it realistically achieve in the future? What are the true potential benefits and risks of this powerful technology? Such as, DNA transfer and use of cell nuclear transfer scientific moral research. Nuclear DNA health science aims to treat disease to assist healthy children. However, human genetic engineering scientists need raise some important concerns that will need to be addressed before any DNA transfer and use of DNA nuclear transfer scientific disease killed treatment to be entered medicine to any patients' bodies decision that can be made on whether doctors should be pursued more thoroughly. Although, DNA cell health treatments has potential benefits, but it has also risks of those genetic engineering now. The new genetic engineering technology is DNA transfer technique designed of the purpose of eliminating disease, which can kill unhealthy cells in patients' bodies by the healthy

DNA cells. For example, disease of heart, liver and kidneys and loss of coordination and muscle weakness. These patients' bad disease cells can be attempted to be killed by the health DNA cells medical drug treatment. However, DNA transfer technology is a attemption of stage, Hence, it has still risk to unsure to enter the health DNA cells to any human's (patient's) bodies. Besides, it has been no offical clinical trial in humans, so trial is illegal. Hence, DNA trafer cell technology is a test stage, so it has risk to patients' bodies if the DNA is unhealth cells. Then the DNA transfer is caused danfer to the patients more seriously, even death risk is possible to occur to patients. For example, when medicine (grug) scientists are carrying on human researching to serve to ensure the safety of new medicine, establish tolerable exposure levels for environment and workplace hazards and determine the effectiveness of new interventions in public health, education and other fields. Without volunteers, these studies would be impossible to conduct. Recognizing society's responsibility to protect human subjects of reasearch from avoidable harm and unethical treatrment. These rules reflects widely accepted principles of ethics. These principles are rooted in values that find expression in many sources of moral philosophy, theological traditions and codes, regulations and rules. They are ethical science or moral science. Due to medical research that poses risk of physical injury rightly. However, the ethical, moral and social issues involve genetic modification , i.e. the direct manipulation of an animal's genetic make-up genetic modification of animals was first achieved with nice in 1980 year, and of cattle, sheep and pigs by about 1985 year. The reasons indicate genetically modified animals are produced include to help scientists to indentify isolate and characterise genes in order to understand more about their function and regulation to provide research models of human diseases to help develop new drugs and new strategies for repairing defective genes to provide organs. And tissues for use in human transplant surgery to produce milk which contains proteins or to alter the composition of the milk to improve its nutritional value for human infants.

In conclusion, in fact, the responsibilities of scientists, who ought to give the corrective scientific reasoning to apply whose ability to scientific community and the broader society, due to who own the nature of responsibility or role generally. Their level of responsibility has minimum demand or ideal to social benefit and who bears the responsibility to the individual or the community of benefits. I think scientists' occupation have the traditional range of research ehtics, or the responsible conduct of research, it is usually concerned over falsification, fabrication, plagiarism and treatment of human and animal and natural and foods and earth etc. subjects. However, I think scientific moralty requires at least four dimensions of consideration to be rules to scientists' behavior. Such as, a set of bases is for the responsibilites; a distination is in kinds of responsibilities; a distinction is between minimally acceptable and ideal behavior and a distinction is between collective and individual responsibility. Thus, scientists need to understand their value of science in society and whose duties are standard complexities in accounts of responsibilities, who need to bear responsibility to carry on researching any new challenges. Moreover, scientists ought need to attempt to answer these questions before who decide to attempt to carry on any scientific researching every time. Is it a general responsibility or a role responsibility? Is it a minimum requirement or an idal? The reason is that scientists need are responsible to rather than responsible for. Because responsibility is for raising problems of interpretation because and ambiguities that reside in that expression. We we say that someone is responsible for something, we could mean that who are be held worthy for something or that it is their ongoing job to take care of something. It combined one thing could be responsible for in either of these senses, makes this a poor starting point for analysis. Hence, if seems have moral and legal overlap to any scientists' behavior, due to scientists are responsible for in particular cases or how public might ensure who are held accountable to people or institutions. In our society, legal and moral overlap is such a map, due to society can't examine the responsibilities of scientists to see if the institutions of science are adequately constructed.

CHAPTER TWO

Drug scientist morality

Supposing you are one medicine scientist in factory.

You need to concern these issues:

How can business managers know that a new industrial process will be , or might be harmful to workers?

If the workers' health problem are serious to cause they can not produce any products. Whether ought business managers get their plant build and working as soon as possible?

Who should be responsible for the health problems in workers created by industrial toxins?

What about problems created in people who live nearly or downwind or downriver from an industrial plant?

What are the most dangerous industrial jobs today of these dangerous jobs and their health and safety risk?

Can you think of any way to reduce those risks?

What are the health dangers of other types of jobs today?

Hence, you moral responsibility needs to know what the new industrial process caused to harmful to factory workers etc. any reasons which related to influence this factory's harmful to workers before you decide to do this investigation. Because you are one medicine scientist, you must need to know what the factors are to influence the harm to this factory's workers, then you need to decide to manufacture what kinds of medicines to reduce their harm to cause their bad health to their bodies in the future. Due to the money spending is very much, if your judgement is wrong to be recommended to manufacture any unused medicines, you will cause your organization to lose much money unfairly. You need to spend time to gather data about how many prior similar medicines are used to the plant workers can be dealt successfully. Then, you need to find what animals can be used to be tested for your new medicines invention in morality. Hence, it is your moral responsibility to your business managers and yourself.

Supposing you are one scientist to carry on researching how to find one kind of drug to kill a wide of variety of disease in the laboratory. You need to find an antibiotic capable of killing a wide variety of disease producing fungi. But the killer you found had to be gentle enough to not harm the human patients it was to be used on. To find this one miracle drug, you had to test eighty different antibiotics each on thousands of dangerous fungi both in laboratory dishes and in live test animals. Do you feel that it is moral to hurt or kill any animals because you need to use these animals to test this one miracle drug's ability whether it can kill a wide variety of disease producing fungi.

Your program consumed over two years of work . It involved over 3,000,000 individual tests and experiments, requires them to grow almost 1,5 million dishes of fungi, and used over 60,000 person hours of work. You hope to explore for additional medicines in the natural environment. Before, you decide to carry on researching this experiments and tests, you need to concern these issues, such as:

What other noteworthy research did you conduct?

How did you get your start in biochemical sciences?

What is fungus?

Eat regularly? Are some beneficial?

Which are dangerous and cause diseases?

Which diseases are fungal caused?

In fact, you need to conducts exhaustive trial-and-error research, testing as many possible fungicides on as many different fungi as possible. Hence, you need have moral judgement to answer these issues, such as below:

i. Animal biotechnology can generate a number of different moral concerns. Distinctions of various kinds need constantly to be drawn in order to pinpoint precisely the grounds of the moral concern and the target at which it is directed. Intrinsic and extrinsic concerns, for example, have to be carefully distinguished as they rely upon radically different forms of argument. Generalisations about the rights and wrongs of animal biotechnology as a whole are not likely to be very helpful.

ii. For moral concerns to carry weight, they should specify what is distinctively objectionable about their target or demonstrate that the objectionable feature is equally objectionable in other contexts. It is illogical, for example, to object to animal biotechnology simply on the grounds that it "interferes with Nature," without at the same time objecting to countless other examples of such "interference" occurring in agriculture, horticulture, medicine and many other activities which most of us accept without question.

iii. A major reason why animals raise ethical issues is that they are sentient beings. Belonging to a particular species does not in itself automatically confer moral superiority or inferiority in relation to members of other species. Taking account of the sentiency of other species may suggest an approach which attempts to calculate animal and human pleasures and pains, or one which respects animals as individuals possessing inherent value .In either case, difficult judgments have to be made about the precise boundaries of the animal kingdom and the qualifications for membership of the moral community.

iv. Moral concerns that animal biotechnology is intrinsically wrong depend largely upon beliefs about its "unnaturalness", but these raise problems of definition and of ethical justification. The question of whether it can ever be right to alter an animal's nature or telos, and if so to what extent and for what purposes has however provoked serious ethical debate.

v. Equally complex and controversial are utilitarian attempts to evaluate the consequences of animal biotechnology in terms of risks and benefits. Huge benefits are predicted by some, particularly in the area of medical research, but these have to be weighed against potentially serious risks. The ethical assessment is further complicated by the issue of animal welfare, and by the question of whether certain levels of harm ought under no circumstances to be inflicted on an animal.

The examples of moral and ethical issues examined in this booklet are not intended as an exhaustive list, though they probably encompass the main areas of current concern. One of the challenges presented by our ever-developing range of knowledge and skills, however is that it continues to throw up novel and more complex questions about what it is right and wrong to do, and these questions cannot be answered by referring back to some previously agreed moral rule-book, partly because no such rule-book exists and partly because, even if it did, it would be inadequate to deal with fresh and often unforeseen developments. Science and ethics, then need to proceed hand in hand in exploring new territories such as animal biotechnology to ensure that the wide-ranging implications for human and animal welfare are kept under constant review.

Hence, your moral judgement is very important to choose which kinds of animals to be tested which is moral.

Supposing you are one medicine scientist to carry on researching in African Jungle. You need to research how to deal with x-ray crystallography and the structure of DNA molecule looks . One of the two great discoveries of your team time in plant DNA genetics.

Your discovery was how the cold cornfield became the base building block for a dozen major medicine and disease fighting breakthrough. You need to concern these issues, such as:

Why study genetics?

What can scientist learn by figuring out how traits are passed from generation to generation?

Why do genetic researchers use pea plants, corn plants and fruit flies to study heredity instead of cooking at people?

Why do you thick some researchers get shoved aside and ignored by other scientists?

How would you feel if you were pushed out of universities and forced to work all alone in a small cornfield?

How do you research the life and work of this scientist?

Why was it easier to figure out ?

What was in a DNA molecule by working with crystals ?

What is a crystal ?

Why don't all scientists cooperate with each other and share information?

What's the difference between competition and cooperation?

You have responsibility to evaluate how to influence your organization fail and your further career development if your DNA molecule research is fail.

You also need to have this medical doctor or physician moral attitude prepare to these researches. Such as, a physician or medical doctor or just doctor is a professional who practices medicine, which is concerned with promoting, maintaining, or restoring health through the study, diagnosis, and treatment of disease, injury, and other physical and mental impairments. Physicians may focus their practice on certain disease categories, types of patients, or methods of treatment—known as specialist medical practitioners—or assume responsibility for the provision of continuing and comprehensive medical care to individuals, families, and communities—known as general practitioners. Medical practice properly requires both a detailed knowledge of the academic disciplines (such as anatomy and physiology) underlying diseases and their treatment—the science of medicine—and also a decent competence in its applied practice—the art or craft of medicine. Both the role of the physician and the meaning of the word itself vary around the world. Degrees and other qualifications vary widely, but there are some common elements, such as medical ethics requiring that physicians show consideration, compassion, and benevolence for their patients. Around the world the term physician refers to a specialist in internal medicine or one of its many sub-specialties (especially as opposed to a specialist in surgery). This meaning of physician conveys a sense of expertise in treatment by drugs or medications, rather than by the procedures of surgeons. Around the world, the combined term "physician and surgeon" is used to describe either a general practitioner or any medical practitioner irrespective of specialty. This usage still shows the original meaning of physician and preserves the old difference between a physician, as a practitioner of physic, and a surgeon. Medicine encompasses a variety of health care practices evolved to maintain and restore health by the prevention and treatment of illness. Contemporary medicine applies biomedical sciences, biomedical research, genetics, and medical technology to diagnose, treat, and prevent injury and disease, typically through pharmaceuticals or surgery, but also through therapies as diverse as psychotherapy, external splints and traction, medical devices, biologics, and ionizing radiation, amongst others. Medicine has existed for thousands of years, during most of which it was an art (an area of skill and knowledge) frequently having connections to the religious and philosophical beliefs of local culture. For example, a medicine man would apply herbs and say prayers for healing, or an ancient philosopher and physician would apply bloodletting according to the theories of humor, but is generally safe when done by an appropriately trained practitioner. In contrast, treatments outside the bounds of safety and efficacy are termed quackery. Medical availability and clinical practice varies across the world due to regional differences in culture and technology. In modern clinical practice, doctors personally assess patients in order to diagnose, treat, and prevent disease using clinical judgment. The doctor-patient relationship typically begins an interaction with an examination of the patient's medical history and medical record, followed by a medical interview and a physical examination. Basic diagnostic medical devices (e.g. stethoscope, tongue depressor) are typically used. After examination for signs and interviewing for symptoms, the doctor may order medical tests (e.g. blood tests), take a biopsy, or prescribe pharmaceutical drugs or other therapies. Differential diagnosis methods help to rule out conditions based on the information provided. During the encounter, properly informing the patient of all relevant facts is an important part of the relationship and the development of trust. The medical encounter is then documented in the medical record, which is a legal document in many jurisdictions. Follow-ups may be shorter but follow the same general procedure, and specialists follow a similar process. Hence, you are as one medicine scientist, you need have close relationship to contact any patients in any places. You need have good moral judgement to decide your any medicines research attempts to deal any harms to your patients carefully as well as you need to decide which kinds of animals to be used for DNA tested is moral.

Supposing you are one brain scientist to carry on researching in medical laboratory. You need to research the therapy of choice for a wide range of mental and emotional illnesses including obsessive disorder, mania and serve depression to achieve to treat patients. You need to concern these issues, such as:

Do you think it is all right to test a new therapy on humans?

Are these some kinds of therapy that shouldn't be tested on humans?

Why are some all right and others not?

How should dangerous therapies be tested?

Whether it is science moral to any death people to use their brains to research the different parts of their brains and the function of each, e.g. how does the brain work? How much does science know and not know about the brain works?

You have moral responsibility to your sample patients or animals to test their brain function by your new medicines invention. People's ethical decision making is strongly driven by gut emotions rather than by rational, analytic thought. If people are asked whether they would be willing to throw a switch to redirect deadly fumes from a room with five children to a room with one, most say yes, and neuroimaging shows that their brain's rational, analytical regions had swung into action to make the requisite calculation. But few people say they would kill a healthy man in order to distribute his organs to five patients who will otherwise die, even though the logic one, save fives identical: a region in our emotional brain rebels at the act of directly and actively taking a man's life, something that feels immeasurably worse than the impersonal act of throwing a switch in an air duct. We have gut feelings of what is right and what is wrong.

In general, brain scientists do not explain why driven the human capacity for forgiveness and revenge, for compassion as well as cruelty, for both altruism and selfish some people fall at one end of the moral spectrum and some at the other. Nor do they explain a related mystery namely, whether it is possible to cultivate virtue through the way we construct a society, raise children or even train our own brains. Hence, you must need to judge whether you need to find who to be tested your new medicine invention to be used how to influence whose brain functions. If you are not ensure your new medicine invention has no any harm to your target testers' brain function for long time. I recommend you ought consider to forgive your target testers attempt.

You are one space scientist to carry on researching in space. Many experiments help NASA engineers to design improved on board systems for the international space reaction orbiting. Earth at the beginning of the 21 ST century, you need to provide essential data for long range planners how designing star ships and space stations the size of cities. You also need to spend more time in space than any other American astronaut, when you need to continue to work in NASA's space program. You need to concern these issues, such as:

How does gravity affect your life?
In what ways do you depend on gravity every day?
You need to keep a one day log of every time you use and depend on gravity to make your life easy and safe.
Did you do anything that did not depend on gravity?
Can you imagine what your same day would be like without gravity?
Where your entry requirement or training any a different from those space scientists.

Due to you aim is that you need to provide essential data for long range planners how designing star ships and space stations the size of cities. Hence, you need to spend more time to gather data about prior long range planners ideas to how designing star ships and star stations. Then you have more confidence to design new space stations and star ships.

Supposing you are one scientist to carry on researching radioactivity to produce new atom. You need to concern, once it was thought to be a molecule. Then, atoms were discovered. Now scientists have opened protons and neutrons and found quarks inside.

What is radioactivity?

What comes out of a radioactive atom?

What happens inside the atom to release this radioactivity?

What is the smallest unit of matter?

If there anything smaller than a quark? What is a quark? What does it look like and act like ? Is exploration of the unknown always risky for scientists?

Do they face suck risks today?

Have they always faced grave risks?

Hence, you have responsibility to find data what the elements of prior atom invention, due to you need to produce new atom, which will have more energy to compare prior atom. However, if you aim to help any one countries' government need to use new atom to attack other countries to cause war occurrence. I think that it is immoral scientific research because you encourage world war in the future. Hence, you need to concern whether what is you atom invention used.

Supposing you are one energy scientist to research nuclear power and nuclear bombs.

You need to concern these issues, such as:

What happens in nuclear fission?

Does fission happen naturally?

How does it create energy?

How do we use nuclear fission today?

What is naturally radioactive element?

What are the others in what ways are they all similar?

What is the difference between natural radioactivity and fission?

If the energy scientist neglects whose morality to research nuclear radiological weapons of mass destruction to manufacture. It will encourage to cause war occurrence difference of different counties in the future. For example, a weapon of mass destruction (WMD) is a nuclear, radiological, chemical, biological or other weapon that can kill and bring significant harm to a large number of humans or cause great damage to human-made structures (e.g. buildings), natural structures (e.g. mountains), or the biosphere. The scope and application of the term has evolved and been disputed, often signifying more politically than technically. Originally coined in reference to aerial bombing with chemical explosives, since World War II it has come to refer to large-scale weaponry of other technologies, such as chemical, biological, radiological, or nuclear. Who can think at this present time without a sickening of the heart of the appalling slaughter, the suffering, the manifold misery brought by war to Spain and to China? Who can think without horror of what another widespread war would mean, waged as it would be with all the new weapons of mass destruction?

At the time, the United States (with help from Western Allies) had yet to develop and use nuclear weapons. Japan conducted research on biological weapons and chemical weapons had seen wide battlefield use in World War I. "It is a very far reaching control which would eliminate the rivalry between nations in this field, which would prevent the surreptitious arming of one nation against another, which would provide some cushion of time before atomic attack, and presumably therefore before any attack with weapons of mass destruction, and which would go a long way toward removing atomic energy at least as a source of conflict between the powers. Nowadays, chemical weapon war will also caused if any biological scientists neglect who morality to use their biological knowledge to manufacture any new kinds of chemical weapons to sell to different countries to gain income to achieve rich goals. For example, after the 11 September 2001 attacks and the 2001 anthrax attacks in the United States, an increased fear of nonconventional weapons and asymmetrical warfare took hold in many countries. The most widely used definition of "weapons of mass destruction" is that of nuclear, biological, or chemical weapons (NBC) .However, there is an argument that nuclear and biological weapons do not belong in the same category as chemical and "dirty bomb" radiological weapons, which have limited destructive potential (and close to none, as far as property is concerned), whereas nuclear and biological weapons have the unique ability to kill large numbers of people with very small amounts of material, and thus could be said to belong in a class by themselves. Such as, Nuclear weapons or nuclear-weapons-usable material or any sub-systems or components or any research, development, support or manufacturing facilities relating to [nuclear weapons]. Chemical and biological weapons and all stocks of agents and all related subsystems and components and all research, development, support and manufacturing facilities. Hence , you are one energy scientist, you have moral responsibility to judge whether your new energy invention would bring more benefits to human or would bring more damage or harm to human if your new energy invention was achieved successfully.

Why do doctors need to concern drug medicine ?

Why does doctor need to consider moral ? Medical ethics is a system of moral principles that apply values to the practice of clinical medicine and in scientific research. Medical ethics is based on a set of values that professionals can refer to in the case of any confusion or conflict. These values include the respect for autonomy, non-maleficence, beneficence, and justice.[1] Such tenets may allow doctors, care providers, and families
to create a treatment plan and work towards the same common goal. It is important to note that these four values are not ranked in order of importance or relevance and that they all encompass

values pertaining to medical ethics. However, a conflict may arise leading to the need for hierarchy in an ethical system, such that some moral elements overrule others with the purpose of applying the best moral judgement to a difficult medical situation.

Instead of being urged to simply "be more compassionate," doctors should learn specific empathy skills during their training to improve their care of patients. According to Dr. David Jeffrey, an honorary lecturer in palliative medicine at the Center for Population Health Sciences in Edinburgh, Scotland, who wrote the paper, there is concern about a general lack of psychological and social support for patients from doctors. Some studies have found that medical students experience a decline in empathy for their patients as they get further along in their training.

In addition, the "commercialization of health care leaves people vulnerable" to being treated as though their care is simply an instrument to bring in money to the system, Jeffrey said. Patients can become dehumanized by the system, he said. But there is also concern that if doctors become too emotionally involved with their patients, they may experience psychological distress and burnout, Jeffrey said.

Jeffrey distinguishes among the three terms that are often used interchangeably — empathy, sympathy and compassion — in an attempt to provide some clarity to this problem. Jeffrey argues that doctors would best serve their patients by striving to have empathy for their patients, rather than sympathy or compassion.For example, having empathy means imagining what it is like to be a specific person undergoing a specific experience, rather than imagining that they themselves are undergoing that experience, Jeffrey said."This more sophisticated approach requires mental flexibility, an ability to regulate one's emotions and to suppress one's own perspective in the patient's interests," Jeffrey told said.

In contrast, having sympathy means taking a more "self-oriented" approach, and imagining what it would be like

for yourself to be in another person's situation.This is a way of trying to identify with a person, but it means that you
assume that people will think and feel the way you do, Jeffrey said. Also, a doctor who attempts to sympathize with a patient may focus on the doctor's own distress, and risk burning out, he said.Having compassion means being aware of the suffering of others, but not necessarily understanding their views, Jeffrey said.What's more, Jeffrey said, compassion and sympathy are simply reactions, that don't involve much reflection.
It takes skill to develop empathy, and developing this skill should be a goal for medical education, Jeffrey said.

In Jeffrey's view, doctors should develop empathy by learning to build a connection with their patients that involves emotional sharing, as well as an "other-oriented" perspective, in which the doctor
tries to imagine what it is like to be the patient. Doctors can then act appropriately on the understanding they have gained to help the patient, Jeffrey said.

"A benefit of this model of empathy is that it focuses on developing skills, attitudes and moral concern rather
than just urging medical students and doctors to be more compassionate," Jeffrey said. "Empathy, unlike compassion or sympathy, is not something that just happens to us, it is a choice to make to pay attention to extend ourselves. It requires an effort."

Animal scientist morality

Supposing you are one animal scientist in the African wild. By the end of summer, you had demonstrated that elephant matriarchs and older made mistakes in identifying familiar from unfamiliar call only once in 2000 times attempts. Matriarchs made mistakes one in three times. The difference in family lifestyle , your work will help African countries improve their national policies and laws regarding elephant matriarchs and elephant herds in general. Elephants live in matriarchal societies. You need to concern these issues, such as:

What does that mean?

Have humans ever created matriarchal societies?

Can you identify and research any of them?

What are the advantages and disadvantages of the matriarchal model?

Why is it important for elephant families to identify?

Do humans do the same thing?

If a stranger walked into your classroom, how would you design if that person should or should not be there?

Is there one person to whom you would look to show you how you should react to that stranger?

Is a classroom like a matriarchal society?

Supposing you are one animal scientist to research in African forest.

How can you find the conducting animal studies?

How many did you find ?

What species did they study?

Where did you find the different between human behaviour and animal behaviour?

What extra problems might you find on learning in a laboratory and African forest differences?

Why are genetically modified animals produced?

You need own animal biotechnology knowledge, such as: In general, the phrase "animal biotechnology" covers many well established procedures of conventional livestock breeding such as performance testing and the use of artificial insemination, as well as major developments in reproductive physiology over recent decades such as in vitro fertilisation (test tube babies) and embryo transfer (surrogacy).Some people would argue that the domestication of wild animals, which began several thousands of years ago, and the selective breeding practices of recent centuries are also examples of biotechnology.

There are five reasons why genetically modified animals are produced:

1. To help scientists to identify, isolate and characterise genes in order to understand more about their function and regulation.

Genetic modification can be used to knock out the activity of a particular gene. By correlating loss of function with this "knock out" it is possible to gain information about the role of the gene and the product for which it codes.

2. To provide research models of human diseases, to help develop new drugs and new strategies for repairing defective genes ("gene therapy").

Animal models of diseases have been used for many years by exploiting naturally occurring mutations in genes, and in-breeding laboratory strains of animals carrying the mutation. An example is a mouse model of Duchenne Muscular Dystrophy. Genetic modification has been used to produce animal models of many diseases including mice with predisposition to cancers, and mice with cystic fibrosis. These models may be made by "knocking out" the activity of genes, as described above, or by inserting defective genes.

By inserting additional copies of a gene into laboratory mice and observing the effects, scientists have recently confirmed the role of this gene in a disorder of human babies that is associated with increased susceptibility to childhood cancers. This will aid the design of new medical treatments. Your moral responsibility, such as,

your work aims to help African countries improve their national policies and laws regarding elephant matriarchs and elephant herds in general.

You need to own animal biotechnology by knowledge to answer above questions, then you can use your answers to assist you to improve new national policies and laws regarding elephant matriarchs and elephant herds more easy.

Supposing you are one animal scientist in an Indian field. This small adventure in a summer bee proved how be bees communicate and just how smart bees realty are. Your work needed to create a more accurate picture of the insect world around us and a better understanding of insect communications. It has lead to a far better appreciation of intelligence and of bees in particular and insects in general.

Why study bees, a more insect?

Why study the lives and habits of any one species?

How does it help human scientists to know how intelligent bees are?

Do you think human tend to underestimate the intelligence of many other species? Why? What species do you think are intelligent?

How can intelligence be tested in other species?

Can you design an experiment to find out research animal intelligence in the library and on the internet?

You have moral responsibility to gather data about prior similar experiments to find out research any kinds of animal intelligence in the library and on the internet, it can assist you to design new experiment to find out research bee intelligence more easy.

● Supposing you are one animal and human behavioural scientist, you need to find whether what animal and human behavioural similarity is and what their difference is. How can you do this research? Whether you need to find which kinds of animals to do this behavioural experiment. If you don't permit any animals to leave your laboratory above one year. Whether do you behaviour is moral?

Then , you can get some methods to prepare to do your research more easy. If you need catch any animals to stay in your laboratory more than one year to observe whose behaviour changing. I feel it is not moral because you control whose free life in the natural environment , due to who will move in your small room , so you need to consider whose free life before you decide to catch any animals to do this research. I feel that you need to gather different kinds of animals and human their prior similar research from prior scientists attempts. So, you can learn how prior scientists do this research before. However, you can gather data about what is human behaviour difference between our old human life 40,000–50,000 years ago and modern human life behavioural changing.

Then , you can find what our human behaviour changing to

compare our animal behaviour changing to conclude what animal and human behaviour changing nowadays.

Behavioral modernity is a suite of behavioral and cognitive traits that distinguishes current Homo sapiens from other anatomically modern humans, hominins, and primates. Although often debated, most scholars agree that modern human behavior can be characterized by abstract thinking, planning depth, symbolic behavior (e.g. art, ornamentation, music), exploitation of large game, and blade technology, among others. Underlying these behaviors and technological innovations are cognitive and cultural foundations that have been documented experimentally and ethnographically. Some of these human universal patterns are cumulative cultural adaptation, social norms, language, cooperative breeding, and extensive help and cooperation beyond close kin. Arising from differences in the archaeological record, a debate continues as to whether anatomically modern humans were behaviorally modern as well. There are many theories on the evolution of behavioral modernity. These generally fall into two camps: gradualist and cognitive approaches. The Later Upper Paleolithic Model refers to the idea that modern human behavior arose through cognitive, genetic changes abruptly around 40,000–50,000 years ago. Other models focus on how modern human behavior may have arisen through gradual steps; the archaeological signatures of such behavior only appearing through demographic or subsistence-based changes.

Archaeological Evidence

In order to classify what traits should be included in modern human behavior, it is necessary to define behaviors that are universal among living human groups. Some examples of these human universals are abstract thought, planning, trade, cooperative labor, body decoration, control and use of fire. Along with these traits, humans possess a heavy reliance on social learning. This cumulative cultural change or cultural "ratchet" separates human culture from social learning in animals. As well, a reliance on social learning may be responsible in part for humans' rapid adaptation to many environments outside of Africa. Since cultural universals are found in all cultures including some of the most isolated indigenous groups, these traits must have evolved or have been invented in Africa prior to the exodus. Archaeologically a number of empirical traits have been used as indicators of modern human behavior. While these are often debated a few are generally agreed upon. Archaeological evidence of behavioral modernity are: burial, fishing, figurative art (cave paintings, petroglyphs, figurines), systematic use of pigment (such as ochre) and jewelry for decoration or self-ornamentation. Besides, Archaeological evidence of using bone material for tools, transport of resources over long distances.

CHAPTER THREE

Computer scientist morality in business

Something radically new is in the air: new ways of understanding physical systems, new ways of thinking about thinking that call into question many of our basic assumptions. A realistic biology of the mind, advances in evolutionary biology, physics, information technology, genetics, neurobiology, psychology, engineering, the chemistry of materials: all are questions of critical importance with respect to what it means to be human. For the first time, we have the tools and the will to undertake the scientific study of human nature.

Computer ethics is a part of practical philosophy concerned with how computing professionals should make decisions regarding professional and social conduct.Margaret Anne Pierce, a professor in the Department of Mathematics and Computers at Georgia Southern University has categorized the ethical decisions related to computer technology and usage into three primary influences:

1.The individual's own personal code.
2.Any informal code of ethical conduct that exists in the work place.
3.Exposure to formal codes of ethics

The concept of computer ethics originated in the 1940s with MIT professor Norbert Wiener, the American mathematician and philosopher. While working on anti-aircraft artillery during World

War II, Wiener and his fellow engineers developed a system of communication between the part of a cannon that tracked a warplane, the part that performed calculations to estimate a trajectory, and the part responsible for firing.[

Supposing you are one mathematician/computer scientist in first mass computer laboratory. You need to design the root language and operate systems for the different computer languages. The first mass produced commercially available computer in world . Besides writing programs, you was a true pioneer in designing and developing whole languages for computers including the most successful languages for computers general purpose. You need to concern these issues:

How is a computer different then a calculator?

What is a computer language?

How does a computer language work?

How does it let us talk to machine?

How can you create a computer language?

Jurisprudence and mathematics are often grouped with the sciences. Some of the greatest physicists have also been creative mathematicians and lawyers. There is a continuum from the most theoretical to the most empirical scientists with no distinct boundaries. In terms of personality, interests, training and professional activity, there is little difference between applied mathematicians and theoretical physicists.

Computer ethics is a part of practical philosophy which concerns with how computing professionals should make decisions regarding professional and social conduct.

Computer morality can include such as:

a. The individual's own personal code.

b. Any informal code of ethical conduct

that exists in the work place.

c. Exposure to formal codes of ethics.

To understand the foundation of computer ethics, it is important to look into the different schools of biology ethical theory. Each school of ethics influences a situation in a certain direction and pushes the final outcome of ethical theory Relativism is the belief that there are no universal moral norms of right and wrong. In the school of relativistic ethical belief, ethicists divide it into three connected but different structures, subject (Moral) and culture (Anthropological). Moral relativism is the idea that each person decides what is right and wrong for them. Anthropological relativism is the concept of right and wrong is decided by a society's actual moral belief structure. Deontology is the belief that people's actions are to be guided by moral laws, and that these moral laws are universal. Utilitarianism is the belief that if an action is good it benefits someone and an action is bad if it harms someone. This ethical belief can be broken down into two different schools, Act Utilitarianism and Rule Utilitarianism. Act Utilitarianism is the belief that an action is good if its overall effect is to produce more happiness than unhappiness. Rule Utilitarianism is the belief that we should adopt a moral rule and if followed by everybody, would lead to a greater level of overall happiness. Social contract is the concept that for a society to arise and maintain order, a morality based set of rules must be agreed upon. Social contract theory has influenced modern government and is heavily involved with societal law. Hence, you need have computer scientific morality to decide whether who are/is your new computer language invention's customer(s) group(s) and how who will apply your new computer language to influence society to bring harms or benefits more in the future.

The first is the recent flu virus that was genetically modified to travel via airborne particles. Basically, a deadly flu virus was made even deadlier. The US government asked the researchers to limit the amount of information is published in academic journals, for fear that the findings would be turned into a flu pandemic. The New York Times has an article on the deadly flu virus. One researcher went so far as to say, "This research should not have been done." In other words, it was not a good thing to even do this kind of research, even if it was done well.

The second example is the trend of personalization in internet websites. This results in "a bubble" around you that only includes news that you want to hear. For example, search engines change their first page of results depending on who is searching. Facebook internally sorts your friends into who you want to hear from and who you do not. This has been explained at dontbubble.us and in a recent TED talk, "Beware online 'filter bubbles'." When a computer filters our results based on what we like, we miss out on things we need to hear. A human newspaper editor can create a balance of different articles on a front page, but a computer filter will only put things that we want to hear. The filtering technology is very good at what it does, but it is not a good tool, as it dulls our thinking and takes away our exposure to ideas we disagree with.

In conclusion, the computer scientist has two roles: to make tools well, and to determine which tools should be made. This requires both technical expertise and a moral compass. It is my desire to see more and more programmers have a moral compass to guide them in their work. Hence, for Computer Scientists, this works on many levels. On the surface, computers are reliable and communicate logically and consistently; they respond in the same way to the same input and give results in a predictable form. People don't; so it's hardy surprising that some prefer one to the other. However, a much deeper problem is how things (possibly including people) actually work. In simple terms, whilst a program might appreciate constant and in-depth analysis, your partner probably won't. Alternatively, if a 'human system' isn't being consistent or reliable, there's a tendency to give up altogether and go back to the comfort of the machine

Reference

Beauchamp T.L. Chikdress & J.F. Principles of Biomedical Ethics (2001). Fifth Edition, Oxford University Press, UK

Gert, B. (1988) . Morality: A New Justification Of The Moral Rules, New York: Oxford University Press, USA

—